TRAVELING GAMES FOR BABIES

TRAVELING GAMES FOR BABIES

A Handbook of Games for
Infants to Five-Year-Olds

Julie Hagstrom

Illustrations by Christiane Stalland

A & W Visual Library • New York

Published by
A & W Visual Library
95 Madison Avenue
New York, New York 10016

Designed by Jane Preston

Library of Congress Number: 80-70373
ISBN: 0-89104-203-2

Printed in the United States of America

*To my mother and father, who showed Amy and Katie
the joy of family travel, inventing new games and
sharing the ones I remember playing as a child on our
family trips of long ago.*

CONTENTS

INTRODUCTION

Going on vacation? What fun! Ah, to be taking off for the wide open spaces of ranch life, the warm summer sun at the beach, or the shade of a mountain pine. Taking the kids? Of course! Families need to get away from the hustle and bustle of everyday life and have some good ol' fashioned family fun. Yes, everyone in our family looks forward to vacation time. Well, almost everyone—I have mixed emotions. I love the vacation once we're settled in, but I dread the long ride across hot deserts or along winding mountain roads it takes to get there. This dampens my enthusiasm because what's the point of a family vacation if by the time you arrive at your destination no one's speaking, or everyone's crying?

I hope this handbook will help many families start and finish their vacations on a pleasant note. I'm surely not the first mother whose heart sinks at hearing "When are we stopping for lunch?" before we are even on the freeway. And of course the animal cookies run out shortly thereafter, followed by the classics "I have to go to the bathroom" (just after you pass the NEXT GAS 70 MILES sign) and, our most popular, "My tummy hurts!" But these universal remarks can be a welcome relief to the squirmy, graham-cracker-covered baby who's trying to destroy her car seat.*

Few of us travel totally unprepared, so at that first sign of restlessness we feel quite confident reaching for the new Scratch-N-Sniff book or wind-up musical radio. But an hour later, doling out one raisin at a time to the baby and "reminding" the three-year-old not to kick the back of Daddy's seat, that confidence is replaced by a tension headache!

Hence this game book for travelers from birth through age four, because if you're like us and don't want to wait "until the kids are older" to take extended trips, you'll need all the help you can get! My husband, Jerry, and I traveled from Amy's, our first daughter's, earliest months, and by the time Katie, our second daughter, was two, we almost knew what we were doing. I hope this book will spare you five years of trial-by-error experience and help you over some of the rough spots while traveling from here to there.

*We have two daughters—what can I say? You're stuck with "she" and "her" throughout the book!

TRAVELING GAMES FOR BABIES

AUTHOR'S NOTE

If you're traveling with an infant under a year old you'll be interested in Appendixes A and B. My two previous books, *Games Babies Play* and *More Games Babies Play,* explain the games we played with our daughters, Amy and Katie, during their first year. Appendix A lists games designed for infants from birth to six months that can be adapted for travel. Before a baby is crawling it doesn't much matter whether she's playing in an infant seat or car seat!

In Appendix B are possible travel games for the baby six months to a year old. I was surprised to find how handy these games were, originally designed for home use, when traveling with eight-month-old Katie. Not wanting to duplicate any of the games in this series (and there's only so much you can do with someone under a year!) the use of an appendix seemed a good idea. I hope this will help those of you in need of a more extensive selection of games for the newborn to one year old.

PART 1

※☓❀☓❀☓❀☓❀☓❀※

Birth to Six Months:
The Sleeping Traveler
(Enjoy It While It Lasts)

As a rule, traveling with a baby up to three or four months old is fairly peaceful. Most infants are lulled by the motion and constant whir of the car and spend a great deal of time fading in and out of sleep. Unfortunately, new parents can't appreciate this easygoing traveler until they've experienced the fifteen-month-old's rebellious spirit!

When Amy was born in June, well-meaning friends told us that this was the summer to travel with her. "It's a snap!" they encouraged. "She'll just sleep the whole trip. *Next* summer you won't have it so easy!" But considering that it took over an hour of careful packing, the entire back of the car full of equipment, and at least three false starts because of last-minute diaper changes just to go for an afternoon visit with a friend twenty miles away, I questioned whether a two-week vacation could be a "snap."

Traveling with a baby does take an awful lot of planning and packing, and if you're used to tossing a suitcase or backpack in the car and heading for the hills, you're in for a shock. This burden of equipment was by far the most difficult adjustment to fatherhood that my husband had to make, and his continuing cry of "Do you *really* need all this stuff?" can still be heard today.

I would like to pass along to you some of the things we learned about traveling with babies.

Where to take a baby under three months old and whether to go at all depends a lot on the baby's temperament and how good ol' Mom feels. Having a baby isn't easy, and taking care of one is even harder, so if you must travel, keep it short and simple. Visiting distant friends or relatives can work out nicely.

A baby up to the age of six months (and older) will ride comfortably in an infant car seat (G.M. Love Seat, for example) asleep as well as awake. We never used a car bed with either of our children, but with our second, Katie, we had one of those lined and hooded straw baby baskets. If you have room for one and can secure it in the car, this works well for very little ones—and you don't need to bring a portable crib.

A Snugglie front carrier is fantastic for the first three or four months (depending on the size of your baby). This is not recommended for riding in the car, but is ideal for museum tours, bus rides, and even restaurants. And the best part is that dads can carry it just as well as moms!

Any assortment of bright rattles or teething toys will keep the baby company from time to time. Musical toys can calm a frustrated traveler, and simple picture books for the three- to six-month-old come in handy.

Following are our favorite games for the traveler under six months old. You don't need to work very hard to keep this age group entertained. Remember, repetition, while it may drive you crazy, is a baby's delight!

❧ 1 ❧
Pinwheel

Equipment: A brightly colored pinwheel. These can be found in most dime stores.

Procedure:
1. Hold the pinwheel out in front of the baby.
2. Blow on it gently, making it spin.
3. Say, "Look at the pinwheel—round and round." Let the wheels slowly stop.
4. Move the pinwheel close enough to the baby so she can touch it. Say, "See the pinwheel. Can you feel it?"
5. Guide the baby's hands in touching the pinwheel corners and stick.
6. Blow, making the pinwheel spin again. Let the baby watch it until it stops.
7. Blow gently on the baby's face, saying, "Blow! Can I blow on your eyes?"
8. Repeat step 7, saying, "Blow! Mommy's blowing the pinwheel."

Variation: Make the wheels spin by rapidly moving the pinwheel in front of the baby. When Amy was older, around five months, she enjoyed putting her hand out to stop the spinning wheels. She was continually amazed at her "power."

❧ 2 ❧
Get a Grip!

Equipment: Any long, narrow objects that a small baby can get a grip on. Try to find things with different textures that will feel unusual to the baby. We used rattle handles, toothbrushes (because the brush part was entertaining too), blocks, Lincoln Logs, and unsharpened pencils.

Procedure: 1. Hold out your first object in front of the baby and say, "What's this? Can you get a grip on this?"
2. Slip the handle (or whatever) into the baby's fingers and encourage her to hang on. You may have to close her fingers over the handle for her.
3. If she gets a good grip on the handle, play a quick tug-of-war game, saying, "Hey! You give me that back!" Just give the handle a gentle pull.
4. Help the baby feel the object's texture or pattern, saying, "Feel the bumps?" or "Feel how smooth?"
5. When she drops it, begin step 1 again with a new toy.

Suggestion: A very new baby, under eight weeks, will need some help in keeping the object in focus. Remember that once she loses sight of something, she thinks it's gone for good!

Variations: The older baby will enjoy a give-and-take exchange with the object. After playing Get a Grip, playfully take the toy from her, pretend to keep it, then hand it back. She'll pick up on the game and want to play too!
Another variation for the younger baby is to move the object slowly across the baby's line of vision and encourage her to follow it with her eyes.

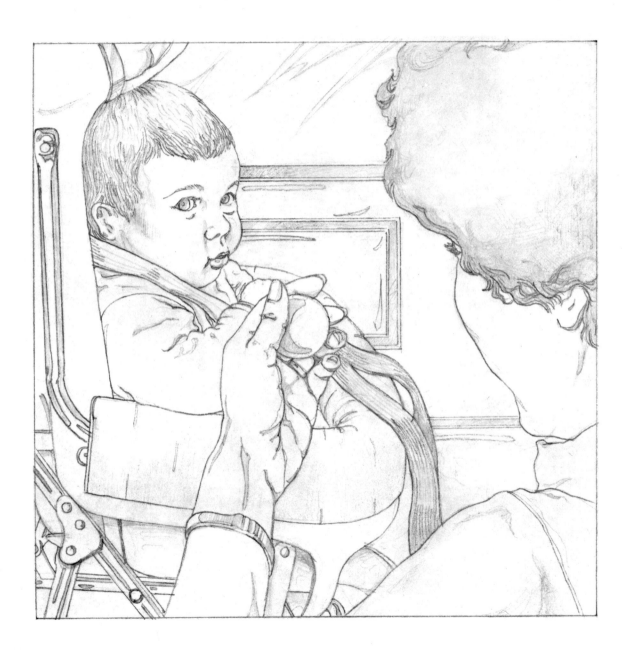

❧ 3 ❧
Now You See It, Now You Don't!

Equipment: Any handy object. We used anything from a tissue to a set of car keys.

Procedure:
1. Hold the object out in front of the baby and say, "See this tissue? Look at the tissue!"
2. Say, "Now you see it!" and then quickly hide the object, saying, "Now you don't!" You can crumple the tissue or hide the car keys in the fist of your hand. If you're using a larger object, it can be hidden behind your back or under your seat.
3. After only a few seconds, make the object reappear right next to the baby. In a surprised voice say, "Now you see it!"
4. Repeat the "Now you don't" hiding routine a couple of times—using the same hiding *and* reappearing spot.
5. After showing and then hiding the object about three times, hide the object in a different place—making it reappear in a different spot also. Above the baby's head or peeking up from under the car seat is a good surprise appearance.
6. Now change objects and begin again.

Suggestion: Using food items, such as cookies or crackers, is not recommended unless you plan on offering them after about two hides. You can't expect a baby, once she's had a whiff of cookie, to concentrate on the game!

Variations: For an older baby (five or six months) the game can be taken one step further by encouraging the baby to seek out the hidden object. You may have to guide her hand to the hidden spot (your fist, perhaps), but she'll enjoy the new twist in the game.

Another twist, one that can really make a baby giggle, is to hide the object somewhere on or under the baby. Slipping a teething ring into a pocket or stuffing it up a shirt is guaranteed to bring laughter (or at least a halfhearted chuckle) from the grumpiest of travelers.

PART 2

Six Months to One Year
The Moody Traveler

The only thing you can be sure of with the traveler six months to one year old is that you'll never be quite sure how she will travel from one day to the next. The first few of these months—the sixth, the seventh, and maybe you can even squeak by with the eighth—are relatively calm. We were lulled into a false sense of security with Amy during these months, and so planned a trip to Yosemite National Park when she was nine months old. If I ever play Pat-a-Cake again, it will be too soon! Alternating between that and This Little Piggy, I lived through the drive—barely.

Many things complicate a baby's life after the seventh or eighth month. Some babies begin to cut teeth, causing all kind of irritation. Some determined types become preoccupied with crawling and want to work on it at all times—which doesn't do much for naps! Others suddenly worry a lot about where Mom is in the car and spend a great deal of time with outstretched arms calling "Mama!" and struggling to get out of the car seat and into your lap. This last trick can drive a normal person to extremes!

But because teeth, crawling, separation crises, and other traumas come and go during this time, you can never be sure if your baby is going to be a content, cheerful passenger or an irrational, impossible-to-please one.

We found with both our daughters that an ideal time to travel was once they were sitting up steadily but not yet crawling. At this point we switched to a Strollee car seat, which seats a baby high enough to see out the window but can also recline for sleeping. Our children seemed to enjoy the view, and once we got where we were going, they couldn't crawl into trouble, not to mention dirt!

It has been said that you learn as you go. Well, here is more of what we learned traveling with Amy and Katie when they were six months to one year old:

If you have room, a "walker" can make your life easier as well as double for a high chair. We also took a portable crib for sleeping. Add to that the backpack carrier and/or umbrella stroller. Let's face it—there's an awful lot of "stuff" (as my husband would say) to take! Starting at about age five months, we used the backpack carrier, and our girls didn't get the bright idea to pull hair or try to climb out until they were about thirteen months. When Amy was ten months old, we planned her afternoon nap in the backpack while we hiked the trails of Yosemite.

You can try taking one of those wooden expanding baby corrals. If your baby is used to a playpen, it could come in handy camping or even picnicking. We never used it for Katie because, to be honest, we never had enough room, what with two kids and us! With Amy we put it around the fire pit and stove—more to keep her out of things than to keep her in.

When packing toys, go through your baby's things about a week before the trip and take out her favorites—squeak toys, rattles, a doll with buttons to fiddle with, or any such thing. It may perk her up to see an old favorite during the trip. You can also buy a few inexpensive novelties—those curling horns you blow at birthday parties or a rubber snake, for example.

Once you get into crackers and bananas, a baby can practically snack her way across state! Whether your baby is eating solids on a regular basis or not, she can still make a teething biscuit last about twenty-five miles. If you keep the sugar content down, your baby will remain calmer. We used to pack a snack kit containing zwieback toast, dry cereal, apple juice (a bottle won't spill), cheese to be cut into small squares, and bananas to be sliced. Be sure to keep paper towels handy.

After the food ran out or Katie was "crackered out," we played the following games through town and country.

❦ 4 ❦

Mr. Magoo

Equipment: A selection of inexpensive children's dark glasses.

Procedure:
1. Put a pair of glasses on the baby and say, "Oh, you look so pretty! Who's our movie star?"
2. Take the glasses off her and put them on yourself. Say, "Look at Mommy, wearing Katie's glasses!"
3. Take them off and hand them to the baby. Say, "Do you want to put them on again?" Help her get them *over* her ears.
4. Let her keep the glasses as long as she's happy. Katie sat back smugly in her glasses with little Mickey Mouse figures on the corners, quite pleased with herself!
5. As soon as she tries to get them off, start over by putting them on yourself.

Variations: Every baby's fantasy—and you may wonder why it wasn't mentioned above—is, of course, to grab the glasses off the grownup's face. Grabbing the glasses off Grandpa kept Katie busy from Baker to Barstow. But let the player beware: When you put on your good reading glasses, you run the risk of having them wrenched off your face. Grandpa had to go to the optometrist before going to work after our last trip!

A couple of cheap necklaces and a hand mirror add to the fun of Mr. Magoo.

❧ 5 ❧
Tap, Tap, Tap

Equipment: Two building blocks, two small wooden spoons, or any other objects that can be clapped together.

Procedure:
1. Holding the blocks yourself, tap them together, saying, "Tap! Tap! Tap!"
2. Hand the blocks to the baby and say, "Can Katie tap the blocks?" You may have to hold her hands and guide her.
3. Repeat steps 1 and 2 until the baby gets the hang of it.
4. Let the baby hold one block while you hold the other. Tap yours against hers.

Variation: If you seem to have lost the blocks (or if they have been hurled out the window), you can get the same effect by just using your hands to play Tap, Tap, Tap.

❧ 6 ❧
Can o' Fun

Equipment: A three-pound coffee can with its lid. Fill the can with an assortment of baby-size items. We used a couple of ping-pong balls, small blocks, small plastic farm animals, and spongy bath toys.

Procedure:
1. Open the can and hold it out in front of the baby saying, "Look at this can! It's filled with fun! Can you find something in here?"
2. When the baby reaches in and withdraws a toy, say, "Oh! Look at what you found! A horsie."
3. There are two ways to play the game from this point. Some babies like to keep pulling toys from the can until it's empty, and some enjoy putting the toys back in the can after each "find." Play it whichever way your baby prefers.
4. Each time a toy is selected, show your baby what it does or says. Show her that a ball can be tossed in the air, a cow can moo or a duck quack. Then hand the toy back to her—either to be returned to the can or stacked on her/your lap.
5. Play as long as she is enjoying herself. You may not get through all the toys. In fact, you'd be wise to save some "fun" for next time.

Suggestions: Two or three one-pound coffee cans may work better for you, and then you'd have extra Cans o' Fun in reserve.

Remember, the objects in the can don't have to be baby toys. Many household odds and ends are intriguing to babies. Just be sure they are not too small to be swallowed, are unbreakable, and have no sharp edges.

Variation: Your baby may enjoy working backwards—dumping all the goodies onto your lap, or hers, and them putting them back in the can.

17

PART 3

✄✕✄

One to Two Years Old
The Rebellious Traveler

This has got to be the toughest time for traveling. I mean, a fifteen-month-old won't even hold your hand or let you change a diaper, let alone sit quietly in a car seat for more than fifteen minutes. Even the most complacent babies begin to assert their independence over the world of grownups. For most toddlers, along with learning to walk comes an almost frightening sense of freedom. They spend much of their time testing this freedom and the rest of their time looking for reassurance that they're still your "baby." So it's not an easy time for any of us—and those supposedly "terrible twos" loom in the not-so-distant future. But, for what it's worth, I love babies of this age. They are so full of life, always amazed at airplanes, birds, and the moon, things that I often take for granted. And they are teetering on the brink of talking—real communication at last! You must admit *that* part is fun! Well, try to remember how you encouraged your baby at this stage, because when she's three you'll be trying to shut her up!

We took several trips with Amy during her second year, and we developed this philosophy: Don't make eye contact! Once she was settled with a book or cracker or for a nap, we would gaze silently out the window while she temporarily forgot our presence. The trick is to stick to a routine and give the impression that you know exactly what to do and when. We once spent a *long* desert drive trying to convince Amy it was nap time. As we sat stoically beside her, she patted (or pinched) our arms, pulled her blanket up over her face demonstrating Peek-a-Boo, and let out periodic shrieks. But, staring straight ahead, we whispered "Ignore her" to each other and continued our vigil. Finally she did drift off.

During an earlier trip I became desperate enough to take Amy out of her car seat—a big mistake. After she had emptied the glove compartment, pushed all the radio buttons, and hung precariously out the window, we knew she had to remain in the car seat. *We* knew it, but Amy didn't agree—wiggling and twisting at the injustice of it all. So my recommendation is, regardless of how deperate you become, be consistent and keep that car seat firmly buckled!

This brings up the controversy over whether or not to stop and let a traveler this age run around for a few minutes before continuing on. I'm afraid I'm not much help on this issue. Common sense tells me it's a good idea—stretch the legs and lungs, get a drink, and return to the car refreshed. But gut instinct tells me it's a mistake. At this age, to be released from car-seat prison and allowed to run free, only to be slapped back into the slammer five minutes later, is a cruel joke. It's a teaser to the baby, who has no concept of time, and doesn't understand that this is *not* the end of the trail! Now, I'm a firm believer in long picnic lunches in a city or roadside park. An hour or so should satisfy those little legs without making a toddler feel gypped after she returns to the car. But you need to try this for yourself because some babies do benefit from a brief jolt of fresh air and a quick game of chase around the restrooms. Need I say, however, that you should *never* stop the car if your baby is sleeping, almost asleep, or even just content? Of course, we always seem to need gas as soon as Katie falls asleep, so be sure to plan ahead!

There are some basic supplies we found useful at this age. In the way of toys, simple picture books are excellent on a long trip. One of Amy and Katie's favorites was Richard Scarry's *Best Word Book Ever*. It takes days to cover all the pages, and the book is fun for older children as well. In fact, when we began traveling with two children, we would pack one box of books, one box of toys, and one box of food. A few puppets and/or dolls will help pass the time, as will a small purse filled with odds and ends (toothbrush, paper cup, toy car, measuring spoons, etc.).

In the way of food, grapes (if they're in season) make a wonderful snack—they are not too messy, are healthful, and can be popped in and out of the mouth for quite some time before being chewed and swallowed.

For a baby under eighteen months you may want to cut the grapes in half to make them more digestible. Graham crackers, cheese, bananas, and Cheerios are pretty safe bets, too.

For drinking we would take a container of plain water. That way no one was tempted to drink too much since it wasn't sweet, and I could mix it with premeasured powdered milk in baby bottles.

Whenever Amy and Katie woke from their naps, finished their snacks, or became bored with their books, we played the following games to pass the time.

19

Bumper Cars

Equipment: A selection of toy cars and/or trucks.

Procedure: 1. Hand the baby a truck, keeping one for yourself.
2. Run your truck slowly along the bar that holds the baby in the car seat. Make car noises—*vroom, vroom.*
3. Take the baby's hand and help her run her truck along the bar. Say, "Here comes Katie's car. Oh, look, it's going to bump into Mommy's car!"
4. Continue guiding the baby's hand until she gets the hang of the game. It shouldn't take too long. Babies this age love the destructive aspect of Bumper Cars, also known as Demolition Derby.
5. Instead of your car bumping hers, make her car slip down the side of the bar in a near miss. Just slip past hers and say, "Oh, you missed me that time!"
6. The game now becomes a game of chase, with her car chasing yours and trying to bump it. All of this activity is taking place on the front of the car seat, or on the baby's legs or knees.
7. After a few rounds, let her have *both* cars and, guiding her hand, encourage her to play by herself. Take advantage of your brief repose; and remember, don't make eye contact!

Suggestion: Be sure to make lots of car noises and crashing sounds to liven up the game.

Variation: If you should forget to bring cars, you can have make-believe cars by using your hands or puppets—even two grapes will work, in a pinch.

❧ 8 ❧
Puppet Surprise

Equipment: You need a mitten-type puppet with a mouth that opens and closes. We had a jolly brown dog puppet with floppy ears and a lolling tongue. A puppet with arms is all right, but one with a mouth is better. You also need an assortment of odds and ends—small cars, small toys, keys, etc.

Procedure:
1. While the baby is sitting in her car seat not looking at you, slip the puppet onto your hand and stick a small object into its mouth, closing it up so the baby can't see it.
2. Make the puppet sidle up to the baby and yawn a big yawn, showing what is in its mouth.
3. Have the puppet say, "Oh, I'm so sleepy today!" Big yawn. Say, "I think I have something stuck in my throat. Katie, look in my mouth. Do you see anything?"
4. Baby will delightedly grab the "treasure" out—Katie couldn't get it out fast enough.
5. Let the baby keep that toy, and put a new one in the puppet's mouth. Turn so that the baby can't see what it is.
6. Sidle up again and repeat step 3.
7. Now have the puppet sidle up, call to the baby, and open its mouth—but the mouth is empty! The surprise here is that there is no surprise.

Suggestion: A little, soft, almost deflated balloon was a favorite with our dog puppet—it made him look as if he was blowing bubbles.

Variation: A puppet can tickle and hug and roughhouse in between surprises, and that will make the game last longer.

23

❧ 9 ❧
Window Wonders

Equipment: None.

Procedure: 1. Strap the baby's car seat next to the window, lock the door, and roll the window down all the way.
2. Let the baby put her arms out the window—they can't stick out very far—and feel the breeze.
3. Lean close to the baby with your arm around her and watch for something of interest to pass by. Say, "See the cow? What does the cow say, Katie?"
4. When the baby tires of passing sights, wave her arms out the window, saying, "Hello, world, my name is Katie, and I am the greatest!" ("Greatest pill," Jerry said of Amy, after she had dismantled the VW bus on the way to Crater Lake!) But, waving to the world, the baby gets some fresh air and exercise, and who knows? she might even get a wave back from kids in other cars!

25

❧ 10 ❧
Quiet Time I

Equipment: None.

Procedure:
1. Put your arm around the back of the baby's car seat and snuggle close to her.
2. In a soft voice, begin talking to her about things she did that day. Use simple sentences and words you know she understands. For example: "Katie threw *big* rocks in the water today." (This was the highlight of her day.) "One, two, three—Katie *threw* the rock!"
3. If you get a response—eyes like saucers, breath held, body stiffening—you know you're on the right track. Talk about anything she has recently done, anything that you know was exciting to her. "And did Katie see a frog? Did you see a froggie?" Pause after each sentence to let it sink in.
4. Now bring in other members of the family by name. "Did *Daddy* go to the stream with Katie? Did *Amy* go?" Continue in a quiet voice as long as the baby is content to sit and listen.

Suggestion: This is an unpredictable age, and if the baby resists sitting quietly—obviously doesn't want to listen—get out a book or something, and wait until she's quieter.

Variation: You can make a song of this quiet talk if the other people in the car can be depended on not to laugh.

PART 4

Two to Three Years Old
The Restless Traveler

When she was two we took Amy to Sequoia National Park. The six-hour drive I was so well prepared for turned into nine hours when our VW bus broke down in the middle of nowhere. I was *not* prepared for that! But ask Amy today what she likes best about Sequoia and she'll tell you the "tow truck rides!" That's what the two- to three-year-old traveler is like—finding adventure and excitement in everything.

You don't need to go very far or look very hard to please children of this age. Katie was our "water baby," and all we had to do was find a creek with rocks to throw and sand to sit in and she'd be happy for hours. If you can still use the backpack carrier, great. Children this age are not really goal-oriented and tend to hike only twenty-five yards before finding a dandy spot to stop. After fifteen minutes or so they may feel like moving on another twenty-five yards, but it's definitely slow going! We worked out a system of taking turns on the trail. First Jerry would speed ahead to see the waterfall or hanging gardens at the end of the hike, then return to us, poking along over tree roots and pine cones. I would then take off for the same scenic wonder, returning shortly to my group, sidetracked by a fallen log. The kids didn't mind missing nature's spectacular sights—they appreciated the simple things more than we did—and were happier setting their own pace. You just can't hurry a two-year-old, and if you try, you'll end up crazy.

But the inside of a car does not hold the wonderful challenges of running water, big smooth boulders, hotel elevators, or trolly cars. So the traveler of this age becomes bored and restless. She's not as irrational as the one- to two-year-old, but she tends to go through her books and snack a little too quickly and then give you a

28

"So what's next?" look. Contrary to my philosophy on the one- to two-year-old, I think that frequent stops are good for this age group. You can set a timer or circle the places on the map where you will stop; it can be as often as every forty-five minutes. The stop is just a quickie—smell the air (dairy nearby?), listen to the sounds (any planes?), and look closely at the ground you've been zooming past (beer cans and gum wrappers?). The spot may lend itself to a short exploration, or your young traveler may want to return to the car and move on. Either way, you've got something to talk about. A stop at a fruit, vegetable, or juice stand can break the monotony, too. If you have to stop anyway, a gas station, while not the cleanest place to wander around, can also be of interest to a two-year-old. Once your traveler adjusts to these periodic leg-stretchers, she'll return willingly to the car—as eager as the rest of you to get to the campsite or motel pool.

We did discover a few new tricks traveling with two-year-olds. For example, those stuffed animals that talk when you pull a cord are fascinating. At two, Amy had just been introduced to Sesame Street and was in heaven with her talking Big Bird. Learning to count from one through ten was a favorite pastime for her at about two and a half and helped pass the time. Don't forget the regular backup of books (an outing to the library before the trip is fun) and dolls to dress and undress (Spiderman or Batman, if you prefer).

In the way of snacks, raisins and nuts can now be introduced. This makes for a much neater car and healthier travelers. A two-year-old can eat just about anything, so take unusual treats that are new to her. Dried apples are great for traveling. Shelled sunflower seeds are a bit salty and slip through little fingers, but mixed with raisins make a new snack. Peeled oranges, eaten a section at a time, quench the thirst and last for several miles.

And between fruit stands and gas stations, oranges and raisins, you might have time to play a few games.

✹11✹
Mommy Says I

Equipment: None.

Procedure:
1. In this variation of Simon Says, you demonstrate the action while giving the direction. Say, "Mommy says: Put your hands on your head," and at the same time put your hands on your head.
2. When your child has copied you, go on to another action. Say, "Mommy says: Put your hands on your knees." Remember to follow the direction yourself.
3. Give your restless traveler directions that will exercise bored muscles. Say, "Mommy says: Put your nose on your toes!" and "Mommy says: Put your elbow on your ear!"
4. When you can no longer think of new positions, let your child be the leader and you follow her directions.

Suggestion: If your child catches on quickly and doesn't need you to demonstrate the actions, just give the directions without demonstrating them. It's fun to see how well your child listens!

Variation: Not all the actions need involve a lot of physical movement. Try directions like "Mommy says: Blink your eyes three times" or "Say 'ho, ho, ho.'"

❧12❧

Catalogue Lookin'

Equipment: Tear out the toy section of any department store catalogue (the Penney's and Sears Christmas catalogues are excellent) and staple the pages together into a book.

Procedure:
1. Sitting close to your child's car seat, place the catalogue "book" in her lap.
2. One page at a time, discuss the toys shown. Say, "Look at the wagons. Do you have a wagon?" Draw to her attention toys she's familiar with.
3. Find a page with a variety of the same toy. Most toy catalogues have an entire page of bikes or dolls. Ask, "Which is the biggest bike?" and "Which is the smallest?"
4. Compare colors next.
5. Once the catalogue has been looked through, you can play a game of choices. Say, "Which would you rather have, a bike or a train set?" (or whatever is shown in the catalogue). Your child's answers may give you new insights into her personality!
6. A good ending to this game is letting your traveler browse through the catalogue on her own.

Suggestions: Some younger children of this age group may enjoy the clothing section of catalogues. You can ask the child to point to, or even circle, shoes, socks, hats, etc.

Variation: Another way to choose favorite toys is to ask your child to rate them. First choice, second choice, and so on.

❧ 13 ❧
Snap 'Em!

Equipment: One box of plastic beads that snap together (such as the one made by Playskool). These can be found at toy stores or even supermarkets.

Procedure: 1. Most toddlers are able to pull these beads apart before they figure out how to push them back together. With the beads snapped together, put your hands over your child's. Gently pulling, say, "*Pull*, Katie, *pull* the beads." Help her pull them all apart.
   2. Covering her hands with yours again, gently help her push the beads back together. Say, "*Push*, Katie, *push* the beads!"
   3. It's best to alternate between pushing and pulling even if it means never having them all together at the same time. Amy and Katie enjoyed this contrast of pushing and pulling.
   4. Once your two-year-old can pull them apart on her own, she may want your help only in snapping them together—just so she can pull them apart again! That's okay—the miles zoom by!
   5. For an older traveler (in her late "twos") you can group the beads by color or design.

Variations: Of course, the finished product will make a lovely necklace or several bracelets for your child to wear.

Our favorite variation of Snap 'Em was discovered by Jerry, Amy's father. In a moment of desperation he squeezed a bead and pressed its hole onto his arm. When he released the bead, suction was created and it stuck to his skin. Showing Amy this feat of magic, he said, "Can you get this off me?" Cautiously she gave it a tug and, POP!, off it came. This was so successful that the rest of the ride was spent sticking beads to noses, cheeks, foreheads, fingers, and even tongues! Our girls were not crazy about having the bead mysteriously stick to them but thoroughly enjoyed snatching it off others!

❧ 14 ❧
School Time

Equipment: A magnetic board (chalk or regular) and an assortment of magnetic letters, animals, or numbers.

Procedure:

1. Begin by showing your child that the letters or animals stick to the board. Have her arrange these in any way on the board. Before introducing a structured game, let her experiment and play around with the board until you sense she's ready for some direction. During a long Christmas vacation drive with two-and-a-half-year-old Amy, she was presented with a Fisher-Price School Days Desk. This is a brief-case-like box with a magnetic chalk board on one side and filled with letters, numbers, chalk, and erasers. She played quite a while independently, and when she was ready for me, this is what we did:

2. Looking down at the letters and numbers scattered on the board I said, "Can you find a blue one, Amy?" As she would reach for the *wrong* color I would cough and mutter "No, no . . . that's red! Oh, I hope she won't pick that one!"

3. When she finally reached toward the right color, I would mutter, "Oh, yes . . . that's it! Get that blue one!" And when she actually chose it, I would say, "*Bong, bong, bong!*" as if she had won a game-show prize!

4. Continue asking her to find certain colors as long as she is enjoying the game. Giving her silly hints and hamming up her correct responses will make the game fun and easy—if she gets frustrated, she won't want to play.

5. Then we would make three groups of letters—each a different color. Amy would move a blue letter into a red group and I would say, "Hey! What are you doing here? You're blue! This is the red group's place!"

6. We would take turns moving colored letters into different groups until, in the end, the "letters" decided that they should all try to live happily together. Is there a moral to this story?

7. You can end the game by putting the letters away according to color.

Variations: If you are using the animal magnetic objects, your child can set up farm scenes on her board. If you have an older traveler who is interested in letter or number recognition, play School Time searching for specific letters instead of colors.

A small felt board (store-bought or homemade) works almost as well as a magnetic board and it's easier to pack. If you use this, you can take extra felt and make up your own game as you go!

PART 5

Three to Four Years Old
The Talking Traveler

Ah, now *this* is the way to travel! Gone are the diapers, the bottles, the portable crib, and the backpack. In their place may be the Hot Cycle, beach raft, and inner tube, but at least it's a change. Here's a traveler who is curious about where she is going, when she is going, and (the three-year-old's biggie) *why* she is going. Be prepared to answer the above inquiries more than once, or twice, or three times. . . .

Go somewhere with plenty of wide open spaces, wild life (squirrels and chipmunks are about as wild as we ever got), and, of course, water. At three and a half Amy hiked alongside her daddy, knapsack strapped on her back, gathering treasures (pine cones and sticks), which she still keeps in a box under her bed. She continues to be an avid collector of treasures today, but her King's Canyon sticks and rocks are her favorites. "Because, Mom," she'll say to me seriously, "they were the first, you know." So enjoy your little traveler and make sure she enjoys herself because these are the trips she'll remember, through photographs, "treasures," and scraps of her own memory.

When Amy was three and her sister Katie six months, we discovered the ultimate traveling convenience—Grandma and Grandpa! If you are lucky enough to pack them in the car with you, you've got it made. "The more, the merrier" really is true when traveling with kids. Our timely rotating of car seats and passengers kept the kids happily distracted and gave the game-weary grownups a chance to relax. In fact, the experiment was so successful we repeated it the next summer! So now you know why this book is dedicated to Amy and Katie's favorite partners in play—Grandma and Grandpa.

But if you don't have the convenience of extra players, here are some new ideas we found useful when traveling with a three- to four-year-old. Take along a clipboard, paper, and crayons. If your child is old enough for coloring books, take them too, but blank paper has more uses. You can teach colors, shapes, and how to draw faces and scribble to the music on the car radio. Marking pens, while they tend to get on face and hands, are thrilling for a child to draw with. The colors come out so bright with just a light touch that even the youngest child's scribbles look lovely. But then you have to keep track of the caps—ours always seemed to slip under the seat—so think twice! We also took Go Fish, any child's first card game. When Amy tired of our showing her how to play it the "right" way, she would have more fun sorting the cards by herself according to color.

I also bought a bag each of cheap plastic zoo animals, farm animals, and dinosaurs. I had intended to use them in the campground, but I found that play dough, packed in a plastic sandwich bag, could be used in the car, spread out over a book to make a great ground cover into which these creatures can be stuck. An assortment of Fisher-Price play people can be used as well.

If you're not too embarrassed, teaching your child simple preschool songs ("Old McDonald Had a Farm") or lullabyes ("Rock-a-Bye Baby") will keep her happy. My problem is that I never know all the words and have to resort to Christmas carols!

When you've played all you care to, for the time being, your child will understand that it's a quiet time for looking out the car window (which is why a car seat is still nice at this age) or napping.

We discovered beef jerky when Amy was three and it was great! One stick would last for anywhere from thirty to fifty miles. Another dandy food item for this age is gum. If you buy sugarless, your child can chew as many sticks as you dare let her swallow. It comes in a variety of flavors, smells, and packages, so pick one of each.

But since all our three-year-old traveler wanted to do was talk (now you know why we recommended gum), we made up the following games to play with her.

✣ 15 ✣
The Finger Family

Equipment: Crayons.

Procedure:

1. Using the crayons, make a face on each of your fingernails. Eyes, nose, and a mouth are all I could squeeze onto my short nails, but add hair if yours are longer!

2. Sitting next to your child, introduce your Finger Family. Wiggle a finger and say, "Hi! I'm the daddy here." Continue with the mommy and three kids until all five fingers have been introduced.

3. Have a member of the Finger Family ask your child, "Say, why don't you introduce us to *your* family?" If she is hesitant, let the finger person guess who is who in the car.

4. Let each member of the Finger Family ask a question. The father might ask, "Where does your daddy work?" and the mom could ask, "Did you brush your teeth this morning?" Let the finger children ask about preschool, pets at home, toys, and so on. Your three- to four-year-old will loosen up and be jabbering away to this "family" in no time!

5. If she wants you to, draw faces on your child's little nails and let her ask you some questions.

6. You can also try having the two Finger Families talk together, although speaking for five different fingers can make one feel slightly schizophrenic!

7. Stage an argument among your Finger Family—two kids arguing over who gets to sit next to the mom. Twist the finger kids around until one of the finger parents steps in and separates them!

8. Continue playing with your Finger Families until your child loses interest or you begin to fade. An easy way to end the game is to let each member of the family say good-bye before wiping him/her off with a tissue.

Suggestions: Crayons on the nails are recommended because they wipe off so easily, but if you want to make a real show out of Finger Family, you can use a pen on the palm side of your fingers, making an entire body. But remember, it'll take some scrubbing to come off.

Variations: You don't necessarily have to have a mom, dad, and three kids. The Finger Family could be an aunt, uncle, and cousins of the traveler, or one of the fingers could be the family pet. Another Finger Family story Amy enjoyed was when we made a baby-sitter and four kids.

If you are really adventurous, and mentally stable, you can use all *ten* fingers for a family reunion. But then you won't be mentally stable for long!

❧ 16 ❧
Ghosties

Equipment: Facial tissues, rubber bands, crayons.

Procedure: 1. To make your Ghostie, crumple one tissue into a tight ball and drape another tissue over it. This will form the head. Wrap a rubber band around what would be the neck, letting the rest of the tissue float freely.
2. Give your Ghostie a face with the crayons.
3. Make several Ghosties, letting your young traveler help you crumple, drape, and draw.
4. Once your Ghosties are assembled, float them through the car, calling your child's name.
5. Since talking is probably your three-year-old's favorite pastime, let her talk to the Ghosties, finding out their names and where they are going. You've got to think fast for this one!
6. Let your child make some Ghosties of her own.
7. Since your Ghosties are more experienced, they can teach your child's Ghosties how to float through the car, saying "Oohhh!" and "Boo!" to the driver.
8. Your child will most likely have some ideas of her own—so follow her lead!

Variation: Ghosties can be played independently—your young traveler whispering to herself as she acts out any number of adventures.

❧17❧

Hidden Doors

Equipment: Apples.

Procedure:
1. Bite a small half circle into an apple. Pull the bitten section open like a door. The skin should be still attached and work like a hinge.
2. Close the "door" and smooth down the skin.
3. Hand the apple to your young passenger and say, "Can you find the hidden door?"
4. Encourage her to turn the apple over and over until she is able to find and peel open the hidden door.
5. Break off the hidden door for your traveler to snack on.
6. Make a new set of hidden doors, being careful to keep the skin smooth, making the doors harder to find.
7. You can continue this game until the apple has been eaten.
8. Then start over with a new apple. This time let your child make the Hidden Doors for you!

Variations: Make your bites smaller and play Hidden Windows! If you're really talented, you can try French, Dutch, or double doors.

  If you have a toothpick, although not many of us make a point of packing them, you can cut faces into apples, almost like carving jack-o'-lanterns!

❧ 18 ❧
Story Starters

Equipment: None.

Procedure: 1. When boredom really sets in, say to your child, "Help me tell a story. Once upon a time, a huge. . . ."
2. Ask her, "A huge what? What should this story be about?"
3. Accept anything she says, from elephant to eyeball. Amy's favorite answer was always "dinosaur." Repeat the sentence using her ending: "Once upon a time, a huge dinosaur. . . ."
4. Now it's Daddy's turn, and the story needs a place. He might say, "Once upon a time, a huge dinosaur lived on a mountaintop."
5. Now it's back to you again, unless you are traveling with more players. To complete the setup, the story needs a problem or situation. Try something like this. "Once upon a time, a huge dinosaur who lived on a mountaintop couldn't find his pet turtle."
6. Once the story is outlined with a character (the dinosaur) and a place (mountaintop) and a problem (the lost pet turtle), let everyone think up the silly adventures that a dinosaur looking for a turtle might have. Take turns telling, and remember to keep repeating as much of the story as possible as you go along.

Suggestions: Your child may want to tell whole portions of the story or just put in a word every few sentences or so. Whatever she's comfortable doing is fine. She'll catch on and want to contribute more to the stories if everyone's relaxed and positive about what she does offer.

Avoid scary or sad stories. Children this age walk a fine line between real and make-believe, and more than once we've brought tears to Amy's eyes or scared her with one of our Story Starter games. So keep it light and funny—lots of cats who play violins and monkeys who wear bowls on their heads!

Variation: For an older player (over four) you can add descriptions (tiny, naughty) and time (in the future, long ago, last Tuesday) to the basic starting setup of character, place, and situation.

PART 6

Four to Five Years Old
The Involved Traveler

The subtitle for this section should probably be "The Finally-Ready-to-Travel Traveler." Our four-year-old studied the map with great anticipation, her imagination running wild hearing talk of crossing the desert at night and getting over the mountain pass. She had several books about the desert and Indians living in narrow canyons or on high mesas, and to think she would visit these places was almost more than she could grasp! Most four- to five-year-olds would benefit from a simple lesson in geography and local history. Many children this age have a very limited concept of their world. Amy was always asking, on the way to the market or Grandma's, "When does the world just stop?" Even after many looks at Daddy's globe, I still don't think she was convinced that the world was round. But no matter, she went on to ask numerous questions about space, stars, and moons, letting us have our silly round-world theory for now.

A child of this age wants very much to be included in grown-up activities and discussions, so don't worry that she doesn't understand everything you tell her; she'll piece together enough information to make her feel involved in the planning and adventure of the trip. I know I learned more about Bryce and Zion National Parks with Amy than I would have without her, because she insisted on knowing all about them.

This age is fun not only because the child is more involved but also because she's a better traveler. With a longer attention span and a wider variety of interests, this little traveler doesn't become bored as quickly as the three- to four-year-old. If your child hasn't already mastered them, you can spend a lot of time practicing these four- to five-year-old skills: blowing up a balloon, snapping the fingers, and whistling.

48

Somehow Amy had the idea that on her fourth birthday she would wake up able to perform these rites of passage and, amazingly enough, she did pick up a birthday balloon and blow it up, but the other feats escaped her. So that summer much of our car travel time was spent positioning thumb and finger into snapping position or lips and tongue into whistling position. Blowing a bubble with gum is another time-consuming skill, but Amy became discouraged with it, stating, "I think you have to be five for this."

Once again, we made a few discoveries while traveling with Amy at this age. Some were good, some bad. First the good.

A small cassette recorder really comes in handy with this age group. You can buy tapes of all the most popular fairy tales and children's stories, along with small paperback books that correspond to the story (you turn the page when you hear the chime). We must have listened to a watered-down version of *Bambi* fifty times between home, Zion, and back home again. And when Amy was tired of hearing these stories, we played a tape of her favorite songs that I had recorded before leaving home. I had chosen just the favorites from her Sesame Street, Mr. Rogers, and *Songs That Tickle Your Funny Bone* albums, and she was delighted. Then—and I'm quite proud of this move—I recorded a Berenstain Bears album I had checked out from the library. Amy was a devoted follower of Papa and Small Bear, and I cleverly packed the books she had that went with the record. Thus equipped, I felt we would never have a dull moment—but of course we did! So we made our own tapes. We brought one blank cassette along, but in desperation you could tape over one of the other tapes. Amy got a real kick out of this. We started out very civilized, singing songs and then playing them back to see how we sounded. But then Amy decided to experiment with more primitive sounds, seeing how many different gross sounds she could growl out! She enjoyed it, we got a few laughs, and the time flew by—and that's what's important, right?

We also found that marking pens, crayons and paper, books, a doll, and card games are still great travel aids.

Now for the bad. If there is anyone in your family who suffers from carsickness, then you'll appreciate our experiences. It's bad enough that my husband is prone to motion sickness, meaning that he does most of the driving and I do most of the playing, but when Amy showed signs of inheriting his affliction (subtle signs like her peanut butter and jelly sandwich lunch reappearing all over the back seat), I felt something must be done. Having supplied myself with a large bottle of liquid Junior Dramamine, I felt confident my problems were solved. We followed the directions explicitly, taking the dose a half-hour before leaving, and Amy never threw up along the windy road down into Zion. Mission accomplished. In fact she wasn't even drowsy—until we got *out* of the car. Since our cabin wasn't ready yet, we decided to take a short hike to a swimming area. Amy whined and moaned that she couldn't walk, was too tired, it was too hot, her feet hurt, and she needed to be carried. Like most mothers, I found this behavior extremely irritating, until realizing that it was probably a belated effect of the Dramamine. Poor kid, she was carried on Daddy's shoulders and survived the afternoon. But I must not be a very quick learner, because we had a similar experience several days later after we had twisted our way out of Zion and arrived at Bryce in time for lunch. The Dramamine, successful again in preventing carsickness, took effect in the cafeteria, where Amy looked at her grilled cheese sandwich, said, "This looks yucky," put her head down on her napkin, and burst into tears! We labeled this dilemma "The Dramamine Connection" and still haven't decided which is the worst fate. So, if you are traveling with a queasy-stomached rider, plan ahead and watch for side effects!

The snack items you pack can include many of the favorites of the three- to four-year-olds—beef jerky, gum, cheese and crackers, grapes. You can also try plain popcorn, but watch the salt, or you'll have awfully thirsty passengers.

By the time Amy had practiced her whistling and listened to her tapes, she barely had time to play games. Nonetheless, here's what we did manage to squeeze in on our trip with Amy when she was four.

50

❧ 19 ❧

Back Tracing

Equipment: None.

Procedure: 1. To get into position, your young traveler can either sit sideways on the seat with her back to you or lie on her stomach on your lap.
2. Start with the letters in her name, or any other sequence of letters she's familiar with.
3. With a straight finger, trace a large *A* (or whatever). Say, "Do you know what letter that is?"
4. If she doesn't guess it right off, trace it again, saying, "It has two slanted lines and a small straight one in between."
5. Retrace only a few times, then tell her the letter.
6. After the letter has been guessed or told, "erase" her back with your hand as if it were a blackboard.
7. Go on to the next letter in her name.
8. When you finish her name, or a word she knows, let her trace on your back.
9. Let your young player trace the few letters she knows how to write (like her name) while you guess them—it's harder than it sounds!
10. If she has difficulty tracing the letters, or gets bored with the same ones, try this: Tell her to draw a face, and you must guess what the different parts are as she draws. She makes a circle and you say, "That's the head!" Two small circles could be the eyes and so on. Remember that a few wrong guesses add to the fun.
11. Now it's back to your turn. Go back to letters or see if she can guess the different parts of the face that you trace.

Suggestion: Remember that the purpose of all these games is to pass the time pleasantly, so don't make them too hard. Some four- to five-year-olds enjoy the challenge of guessing letters, while others become frustrated.

Variations: Having letters or faces traced on your back is a very pleasant feeling. If your child feels lazy, you can switch the game to a good back scratching or rubbing session. Be sure to get your turn—Ahhh!

Not only letters or faces can be traced and guessed, but numbers, animal drawings, or shapes.

53

⚜ 20 ⚜
Quiet Time II

Equipment: None.

Procedure:
1. Snuggling close to your child, begin speaking in a quiet tone. Say, "Gosh, we haven't seen your room for so long!"
2. Continue, creating a mental picture of her room. "Okay, let's pretend we are opening your door. Are there any pictures on your door?"
3. Talk about what is the first thing she sees—colors on her bed, posters on the wall, etc.
4. By asking specific questions, let her describe her room and the things in it.
5. If she is still in a Quiet Time mood, go on to discuss the outside yard or another favorite play place.

Suggestion: As with Quiet Time I, if your traveler is too restless to settle down, don't make an issue out of it—try again later.

Variations: There are any number of situations or places you can re-create during Quiet Time. For example, talk about what you've done that day, or what the cabin, motel, or campsite looked like.

Using a puppet to talk with your child during Quiet Time is fun and a change of pace. We had a dog puppet who "talked" to Amy, and she enjoyed telling him all about her room at home.

On your first day of travel, the puppet can ask all kinds of questions about what it will be like and what there is to do on vacation. Amy's dog puppet was very concerned about what dogs could do there and was crushed when Amy told him he couldn't go horseback riding!

❧ 21 ❧

On the Lookout!

Equipment: None.

Procedure:
1. The player starting the game says, "I'm looking for a yellow car."
2. Other players in the car then are On the Lookout for a yellow car. It may be found on the freeway, sidestreets, or bridges you speed past.
3. Whoever sees the yellow car calls out and points to her discovery, letting the other players verify the "find."
4. The player who wins this round is the one who gets to choose what to be On the Lookout for in the next round. Amy was interested in campers, and when it was her turn to choose, we would all have to look for some form of rolling home.
5. Continue the game, the winner choosing what to be looking for the next time.

Suggestion: A young traveler who rarely gets a chance to win will become discouraged. You'll have to be the judge of when to help her win and when to let her lose. Upon spying the searched-for vehicle ourselves, we used to give Amy subtle hints like "I'll bet a blue truck will be coming across the bridge any minute" when we felt she was losing interest.

Variations: Depending on the age of the players, On the Lookout can become quite complex— looking for a blue van with three different colored stripes, or a camper pulling a boat.
   If you are in farm country, you can look for cows, barns, tractors, or horses. And in the city you can be On the Lookout for banks, buses, or skyscrapers.

57

❧ **22** ❧

Card Shark I

Equipment: At least one deck of playing cards.

Procedure: 1. Remove the jokers, kings, queens, jacks, and aces from the decks.
2. An easy card game for a four- to five-year-old is War or Battle. To play, divide one deck in half between two players, or use two decks.
3. Keeping your stacks of cards face down, you each draw one card at a time and flip them face up side by side.
4. The player with the higher card wins them both.
5. Make the game exciting by counting. "One, two, three, FLIP!" This builds up dramatically to the final flip of the cards, revealing their numbers.
6. Continue on, flipping over the next card of each stack. After the cards have been flipped over, ask your young player to identify the numbers and name the higher card.
7. In case of a tie, flip two more cards, the higher card winning all four.
8. The player with the most cards collected at the end of the game is the winner.

Suggestion: A big buildup to the "FLIP" part is a must to keep the game exciting.

Variation: Add the kings or queens, and if they flip up it's a sure win or a sure loss—whichever way appeals to your child.

⚜23⚜
Card Shark II

Equipment: At least one deck of playing cards.

Procedure: 1. Another card game that's fun to play in the car is a simplification of Concentration. To play, lay four to six cards face up on a book, magazine, or pillow.
2. Say to your child, "Look at these cards carefully because I'm going to take one away and you have to guess which one!"
3. You can go over the cards with your child to make sure she knows them.
4. Your young player then closes her eyes and you remove a card.
5. When you say "Ready!" she opens her eyes and guesses which card has been taken away.
6. Depending on your child, give as many hints as you need to keep the game fun for her.
7. Repeat steps 3 and 4, removing a different card.
8. Now let your partner remove the card and you guess which one is missing. Remember, don't make it look too easy, but don't play dumb either.

Suggestions: To make it easy in the beginning, use the same color cards in a sequence. Then use one row of red in a sequence and one row of black in a sequence.

Leave a space where the card was removed, and don't switch the cards around.

Variations: You can teach your phone number this way, as long as you haven't any zeros or ones in your number!

If your child is enjoying the game, you can gradually make it more difficult—use numbers out of a sequence or add more cards.

Concentration-type games don't have to be played with cards. Having left the cards at the motel, we once played the game with toy trucks, guessing which of the five was missing. Money can be used, too, or even food!

61

❧24❧
Keep a Stiff Upper Lip

Equipment: None.

Procedure:
1. Sitting beside your child, say, "I'll bet you can't make me laugh by tickling me."
2. Few children will pass up such a challenge, the response usually being, "Oh, I bet I can!"
3. Let her reach over and tickle under your chin, your ribs, or wherever she can reach.
4. Meanwhile you pretend to be holding back hysterical laughter by squirming and rolling your eyes around in your head!
5. Finally she tickles a sensitive spot and you burst out laughing. Say, "Oh! You did it! I just couldn't hold it in any longer."
6. Now it's your turn to tickle her. Say, "Now don't laugh! See how long *you* can go without laughing!" When Amy played, suggesting she not laugh and then slowly reaching over for the tickle brought on hysterics before she was even touched!
7. Let your traveler have several turns in a row, trying to Keep a Stiff Upper Lip, and she'll get better at controlling herself.
8. Continue taking turns until everyone is tickled out.

Variation: Try playing Keep a Stiff Upper Lip making funny faces instead of tickling. Your little traveler will probably come up with some wild faces hard to resist laughing at!

❧ 25 ❧

I Follow the Eye

Equipment: None.

Procedure:
1. To begin the game, stare at an object in the car and say, "I'm looking at something red" (or whatever color it is).
2. As the other player(s) look frantically around to find something red, you say, "Look where I am looking. You have to follow my eyes!"
3. While you keep your eyes focused on the object, your young player must follow the direct line of your gaze (with her finger if necessary) in order to identify the object.
4. If she names the wrong item, say, "Am I looking over there?" Shift your stare to the wrong place to illustrate that you were *not* looking in that direction.
5. Again, say, "Follow my eyes to something red."
6. When she finally guesses it, then it's her turn to pick an object for you to find. You will have to remind her to keep her eyes on the object in question. Amy thought that just stretching her eyes as wide as possible was good enough—the eyes themselves darted from dashboard to door!
7. Continue taking turns following the eyes to secret spots.

Suggestions: It's best to guess your partner's chosen object after a few false tries. This gives *her* a chance to explain that *her* eyes are not looking that way!

Choosing things *outside* the car does not work, for obvious reasons—although Amy thought this was very clever and, when we would finally give up on her, "something blue," she would tell us it was a sign we passed ten miles ago!

This game works very well in restaurants. In fact, we played it more often waiting for food than we did in the car.

Variation: As your child becomes more proficient, you may have to pick harder objects or limit her number of guesses.

❧ 26 ❧
Mommy Says II

Equipment: None.

Procedure:
1. To distract a restless traveler during that last stretch of miles, suddenly say, "Mommy says: Clap your hands, then touch your knees!"
2. Your child will have to think twice about these directions, so give her a few minutes.
3. After she follows these directions, give her a new set—"Mommy says: Blink your eyes and then wiggle your toes."
4. As your child catches on to the game, add even another direction in your next Mommy Says— perhaps "Touch your nose, then kiss your hand, and then stick out your tongue."
5. After a few of these, let your partner give you the directions, playing "Amy says. . . ."
6. When it's your turn to give the directions, try telling her *how many* times to do something. Say, "Mommy says: Clap your hands three times and then blink your eyes two times."
7. Continue taking turns until interest fades.

Suggestions: When telling your partner how many times to do something, be sure she knows how many times to do each separate action. When told to clap her hands three times, then blink her eyes, Amy would also blink three times!

Remember to keep your directions simple and clear—your child will take you literally!

Variations: If you are traveling with an extrordinarly well-coordinated player, she can try doing all the actions at once, instead of one at a time.

CONCLUSION

I think the single most important lesson we've learned throughout our travels is organization, because *where* you pack things is almost as important as *what* things you pack. If you can reach down and pull an apple from the box at your feet to calm a restless passenger, things will go a lot more smoothly than if you have to pull the car over on a busy highway to get the cooler out of the trunk, or even worse, off the rack! Even if you have the convenience of a van-type car, you should still keep the basic travel needs close at hand—and *your* hand at that!

The food box or cooler must be especially well protected from small investigative fingers. Rationing snacks with an element of surprise is crucial in distracting weary travelers. Don't shoot your whole wad in the first fifty miles! The same holds true of toys. Smuggle in one or two new items, and you be the judge of when they're needed the most.

Just as you plan the clothes you'll wear on vacation, decide in advance what games you'll play and pack any needed equipment. Space the games out, only playing when you have to.

After all is said and done, you may choose to hire a sitter and leave the kids at home! It's true that parents need time to themselves, and you ought to get away at least once a year. But, if you're like us, you spend most of your vacation talking about the kids, phoning the kids, and buying corny souvenirs for the kids! We usually spend a lot of time watching other people's children, guessing their ages, and saying, "Oh, Amy would have loved this!" or "Katie would've had a blast here!" even when we know that our antique-filled hotel or three-hour museum tour wouldn't have been suitable for children.

On the way home we discuss our next vacation, this time with the kids. I gaze out the window or read my book in peace and quiet and wonder, am I nuts? This is heaven! But, what can I say, we miss the spontaneous fun, the easy excitement and breathless joy that our children bring with them on our carefully planned kid-oriented trips. It's our hope that by sharing our experiences and games with you, your family travels will be easier this time and looked forward to in the future.

APPENDIX A

From *Games Babies Play*:
   Follow the Face
   Mirror, Mirror
   Mousie
   What's the Diff
   What's the Diff II
   Reach for the Sky
   Peek-a-Boo
   Gotcha
   Story Time

From *More Games Babies Play*:
   Now Hear This
   Eye to Eye
   Snap 'N' Clap
   Driver Training
   Shadow Shapes
   Indian Chants
   Tell Me About It
   Hands Down
   Bug Patrol
   Go for the Toe

APPENDIX B

From *Games Babies Play*:
- Pat-a-Cake
- Backwards Peek-a-Boo
- Grab It!
- Animal Introductions
- Puppet Play
- Sing-a-Long
- Put In—Take Away
- Story Time II

From *More Games Babies Play*:
- Tiger Roar
- Be My Echo
- Bzzzt!
- Can It!
- Ring, Ring!
- Sweet Lovin'